LOG
BOOK CORNER
best journal for you

Name: ....

Phone: ....

Cell: ....

Email: ....

Company: ....

Street: ....

City: ....

State: ....

Zip: ....

THIS BOOK BELONGS TO:

____

____

____

____

____

____

____

Web Site:
Username:
Email Used:
Password(s):

Notes/Security Question/Hint:

Web Site:
Username:
Email Used:
Password(s):

Notes/Security Question/Hint:

Web Site:
Username:
Email Used:
Password(s):

Notes/Security Question/Hint:

Web Site:
Username:
Email Used:
Password(s):
Notes/Security Question/Hint:

Web Site:
Username:
Email Used:
Password(s):
Notes/Security Question/Hint:

Web Site:
Username:
Email Used:
Password(s):
Notes/Security Question/Hint:

Web Site:
Username:
Email Used:
Password(s):
Notes/Security Question/Hint:

Web Site:
Username:
Email Used:
Password(s):
Notes/Security Question/Hint:

Web Site:
Username:
Email Used:
Password(s):
Notes/Security Question/Hint:

Web Site:
Username:
Email Used:
Password(s):

Notes/Security Question/Hint:

Web Site:
Username:
Email Used:
Password(s):

Notes/Security Question/Hint:

Web Site:
Username:
Email Used:
Password(s):

Notes/Security Question/Hint:

Web Site:
Username:
Email Used:
Password(s):
Notes/Security Question/Hint:

Web Site:
Username:
Email Used:
Password(s):
Notes/Security Question/Hint:

Web Site:
Username:
Email Used:
Password(s):
Notes/Security Question/Hint:

Web Site:
Username:
Email Used:
Password(s):

Notes/Security Question/Hint:

Web Site:
Username:
Email Used:
Password(s):

Notes/Security Question/Hint:

Web Site:
Username:
Email Used:
Password(s):

Notes/Security Question/Hint:

Web Site:
Username:
Email Used:
Password(s):
Notes/Security Question/Hint:

Web Site:
Username:
Email Used:
Password(s):
Notes/Security Question/Hint:

Web Site:
Username:
Email Used:
Password(s):
Notes/Security Question/Hint:

Web Site:
Username:
Email Used:
Password(s):

Notes/Security Question/Hint:

Web Site:
Username:
Email Used:
Password(s):

Notes/Security Question/Hint:

Web Site:
Username:
Email Used:
Password(s):

Notes/Security Question/Hint:

Web Site:
Username:
Email Used:
Password(s):
Notes/Security Question/Hint:

Web Site:
Username:
Email Used:
Password(s):
Notes/Security Question/Hint:

Web Site:
Username:
Email Used:
Password(s):
Notes/Security Question/Hint:

Web Site:	
Username:	
Email Used:	
Password(s):	
Notes/Security Question/Hint:	

Web Site:	
Username:	
Email Used:	
Password(s):	
Notes/Security Question/Hint:	

Web Site:	
Username:	
Email Used:	
Password(s):	
Notes/Security Question/Hint:	

Web Site:
Username:
Email Used:
Password(s):
Notes/Security Question/Hint:

Web Site:
Username:
Email Used:
Password(s):
Notes/Security Question/Hint:

Web Site:
Username:
Email Used:
Password(s):
Notes/Security Question/Hint:

Web Site:
Username:
Email Used:
Password(s):

Notes/Security Question/Hint:

Web Site:
Username:
Email Used:
Password(s):

Notes/Security Question/Hint:

Web Site:
Username:
Email Used:
Password(s):

Notes/Security Question/Hint:

Web Site:
Username:
Email Used:
Password(s):
Notes/Security Question/Hint:

Web Site:
Username:
Email Used:
Password(s):
Notes/Security Question/Hint:

Web Site:
Username:
Email Used:
Password(s):
Notes/Security Question/Hint:

Web Site:
Username:
Email Used:
Password(s):
Notes/Security Question/Hint:

Web Site:
Username:
Email Used:
Password(s):
Notes/Security Question/Hint:

Web Site:
Username:
Email Used:
Password(s):
Notes/Security Question/Hint:

Web Site:
Username:
Email Used:
Password(s):
Notes/Security Question/Hint:

Web Site:
Username:
Email Used:
Password(s):
Notes/Security Question/Hint:

Web Site:
Username:
Email Used:
Password(s):
Notes/Security Question/Hint:

Web Site:
Username:
Email Used:
Password(s):
Notes/Security Question/Hint:

Web Site:
Username:
Email Used:
Password(s):
Notes/Security Question/Hint:

Web Site:
Username:
Email Used:
Password(s):
Notes/Security Question/Hint:

Web Site:
Username:
Email Used:
Password(s):
Notes/Security Question/Hint:

Web Site:
Username:
Email Used:
Password(s):
Notes/Security Question/Hint:

Web Site:
Username:
Email Used:
Password(s):
Notes/Security Question/Hint:

Web Site:
Username:
Email Used:
Password(s):
Notes/Security Question/Hint:

Web Site:
Username:
Email Used:
Password(s):
Notes/Security Question/Hint:

Web Site:
Username:
Email Used:
Password(s):
Notes/Security Question/Hint:

Web Site:
Username:
Email Used:
Password(s):
Notes/Security Question/Hint:

Web Site:
Username:
Email Used:
Password(s):
Notes/Security Question/Hint:

Web Site:
Username:
Email Used:
Password(s):
Notes/Security Question/Hint:

Web Site:
Username:
Email Used:
Password(s):
Notes/Security Question/Hint:

Web Site:
Username:
Email Used:
Password(s):
Notes/Security Question/Hint:

Web Site:
Username:
Email Used:
Password(s):
Notes/Security Question/Hint:

Web Site:
Username:
Email Used:
Password(s):
Notes/Security Question/Hint:

Web Site:
Username:
Email Used:
Password(s):
Notes/Security Question/Hint:

Web Site:
Username:
Email Used:
Password(s):
Notes/Security Question/Hint:

Web Site:
Username:
Email Used:
Password(s):

Notes/Security Question/Hint:

Web Site:
Username:
Email Used:
Password(s):

Notes/Security Question/Hint:

Web Site:
Username:
Email Used:
Password(s):

Notes/Security Question/Hint:

Web Site:
Username:
Email Used:
Password(s):

Notes/Security Question/Hint:

Web Site:
Username:
Email Used:
Password(s):

Notes/Security Question/Hint:

Web Site:
Username:
Email Used:
Password(s):

Notes/Security Question/Hint:

Web Site:
Username:
Email Used:
Password(s):
Notes/Security Question/Hint:

Web Site:
Username:
Email Used:
Password(s):
Notes/Security Question/Hint:

Web Site:
Username:
Email Used:
Password(s):
Notes/Security Question/Hint:

Web Site:
Username:
Email Used:
Password(s):
Notes/Security Question/Hint:

Web Site:
Username:
Email Used:
Password(s):
Notes/Security Question/Hint:

Web Site:
Username:
Email Used:
Password(s):
Notes/Security Question/Hint:

Web Site:
Username:
Email Used:
Password(s):
Notes/Security Question/Hint:

Web Site:
Username:
Email Used:
Password(s):
Notes/Security Question/Hint:

Web Site:
Username:
Email Used:
Password(s):
Notes/Security Question/Hint:

Web Site:
Username:
Email Used:
Password(s):
Notes/Security Question/Hint:

Web Site:
Username:
Email Used:
Password(s):
Notes/Security Question/Hint:

Web Site:
Username:
Email Used:
Password(s):
Notes/Security Question/Hint:

Web Site:
Username:
Email Used:
Password(s):

Notes/Security Question/Hint:

Web Site:
Username:
Email Used:
Password(s):

Notes/Security Question/Hint:

Web Site:
Username:
Email Used:
Password(s):

Notes/Security Question/Hint:

Web Site:
Username:
Email Used:
Password(s):
Notes/Security Question/Hint:

Web Site:
Username:
Email Used:
Password(s):
Notes/Security Question/Hint:

Web Site:
Username:
Email Used:
Password(s):
Notes/Security Question/Hint:

Web Site:
Username:
Email Used:
Password(s):
Notes/Security Question/Hint:

Web Site:
Username:
Email Used:
Password(s):
Notes/Security Question/Hint:

Web Site:
Username:
Email Used:
Password(s):
Notes/Security Question/Hint:

Web Site:
Username:
Email Used:
Password(s):
Notes/Security Question/Hint:

Web Site:
Username:
Email Used:
Password(s):
Notes/Security Question/Hint:

Web Site:
Username:
Email Used:
Password(s):
Notes/Security Question/Hint:

Web Site:

Username:

Email Used:

Password(s):

Notes/Security Question/Hint:

Web Site:

Username:

Email Used:

Password(s):

Notes/Security Question/Hint:

Web Site:

Username:

Email Used:

Password(s):

Notes/Security Question/Hint:

Web Site:
Username:
Email Used:
Password(s):
Notes/Security Question/Hint:

Web Site:
Username:
Email Used:
Password(s):
Notes/Security Question/Hint:

Web Site:
Username:
Email Used:
Password(s):
Notes/Security Question/Hint:

Web Site:
Username:
Email Used:
Password(s):
Notes/Security Question/Hint:

Web Site:
Username:
Email Used:
Password(s):
Notes/Security Question/Hint:

Web Site:
Username:
Email Used:
Password(s):
Notes/Security Question/Hint:

Web Site:
Username:
Email Used:
Password(s):
Notes/Security Question/Hint:

Web Site:
Username:
Email Used:
Password(s):
Notes/Security Question/Hint:

Web Site:
Username:
Email Used:
Password(s):
Notes/Security Question/Hint:

Web Site:
Username:
Email Used:
Password(s):
Notes/Security Question/Hint:

Web Site:
Username:
Email Used:
Password(s):
Notes/Security Question/Hint:

Web Site:
Username:
Email Used:
Password(s):
Notes/Security Question/Hint:

Web Site:
Username:
Email Used:
Password(s):
Notes/Security Question/Hint:

Web Site:
Username:
Email Used:
Password(s):
Notes/Security Question/Hint:

Web Site:
Username:
Email Used:
Password(s):
Notes/Security Question/Hint:

Web Site:

Username:

Email Used:

Password(s):

Notes/Security Question/Hint:

Web Site:

Username:

Email Used:

Password(s):

Notes/Security Question/Hint:

Web Site:

Username:

Email Used:

Password(s):

Notes/Security Question/Hint:

Web Site:
Username:
Email Used:
Password(s):
Notes/Security Question/Hint:

Web Site:
Username:
Email Used:
Password(s):
Notes/Security Question/Hint:

Web Site:
Username:
Email Used:
Password(s):
Notes/Security Question/Hint:

Web Site:
Username:
Email Used:
Password(s):
Notes/Security Question/Hint:

Web Site:
Username:
Email Used:
Password(s):
Notes/Security Question/Hint:

Web Site:
Username:
Email Used:
Password(s):
Notes/Security Question/Hint:

Web Site:
Username:
Email Used:
Password(s):
Notes/Security Question/Hint:

Web Site:
Username:
Email Used:
Password(s):
Notes/Security Question/Hint:

Web Site:
Username:
Email Used:
Password(s):
Notes/Security Question/Hint:

Web Site:
Username:
Email Used:
Password(s):
Notes/Security Question/Hint:

Web Site:
Username:
Email Used:
Password(s):
Notes/Security Question/Hint:

Web Site:
Username:
Email Used:
Password(s):
Notes/Security Question/Hint:

Web Site:
Username:
Email Used:
Password(s):
Notes/Security Question/Hint:

Web Site:
Username:
Email Used:
Password(s):
Notes/Security Question/Hint:

Web Site:
Username:
Email Used:
Password(s):
Notes/Security Question/Hint:

Web Site:
Username:
Email Used:
Password(s):
Notes/Security Question/Hint:

Web Site:
Username:
Email Used:
Password(s):
Notes/Security Question/Hint:

Web Site:
Username:
Email Used:
Password(s):
Notes/Security Question/Hint:

Web Site:
Username:
Email Used:
Password(s):
Notes/Security Question/Hint:

Web Site:
Username:
Email Used:
Password(s):
Notes/Security Question/Hint:

Web Site:
Username:
Email Used:
Password(s):
Notes/Security Question/Hint:

Web Site:
Username:
Email Used:
Password(s):

Notes/Security Question/Hint:

Web Site:
Username:
Email Used:
Password(s):

Notes/Security Question/Hint:

Web Site:
Username:
Email Used:
Password(s):

Notes/Security Question/Hint:

<table>
<tr><td>Web Site:</td></tr>
<tr><td>Username:</td></tr>
<tr><td>Email Used:</td></tr>
<tr><td>Password(s):</td></tr>
<tr><td></td></tr>
<tr><td></td></tr>
<tr><td>Notes/Security Question/Hint:</td></tr>
<tr><td></td></tr>
<tr><td></td></tr>
<tr><td></td></tr>
</table>

<table>
<tr><td>Web Site:</td></tr>
<tr><td>Username:</td></tr>
<tr><td>Email Used:</td></tr>
<tr><td>Password(s):</td></tr>
<tr><td></td></tr>
<tr><td></td></tr>
<tr><td>Notes/Security Question/Hint:</td></tr>
<tr><td></td></tr>
<tr><td></td></tr>
<tr><td></td></tr>
</table>

<table>
<tr><td>Web Site:</td></tr>
<tr><td>Username:</td></tr>
<tr><td>Email Used:</td></tr>
<tr><td>Password(s):</td></tr>
<tr><td></td></tr>
<tr><td></td></tr>
<tr><td>Notes/Security Question/Hint:</td></tr>
<tr><td></td></tr>
<tr><td></td></tr>
<tr><td></td></tr>
</table>

Web Site:
Username:
Email Used:
Password(s):
Notes/Security Question/Hint:

Web Site:
Username:
Email Used:
Password(s):
Notes/Security Question/Hint:

Web Site:
Username:
Email Used:
Password(s):
Notes/Security Question/Hint:

Web Site:
Username:
Email Used:
Password(s):
Notes/Security Question/Hint:

Web Site:
Username:
Email Used:
Password(s):
Notes/Security Question/Hint:

Web Site:
Username:
Email Used:
Password(s):
Notes/Security Question/Hint:

Web Site:

Username:

Email Used:

Password(s):

Notes/Security Question/Hint:

Web Site:

Username:

Email Used:

Password(s):

Notes/Security Question/Hint:

Web Site:

Username:

Email Used:

Password(s):

Notes/Security Question/Hint:

Web Site:
Username:
Email Used:
Password(s):
Notes/Security Question/Hint:

Web Site:
Username:
Email Used:
Password(s):
Notes/Security Question/Hint:

Web Site:
Username:
Email Used:
Password(s):
Notes/Security Question/Hint:

Web Site:
Username:
Email Used:
Password(s):
Notes/Security Question/Hint:

Web Site:
Username:
Email Used:
Password(s):
Notes/Security Question/Hint:

Web Site:
Username:
Email Used:
Password(s):
Notes/Security Question/Hint:

Web Site:
Username:
Email Used:
Password(s):
Notes/Security Question/Hint:

Web Site:
Username:
Email Used:
Password(s):
Notes/Security Question/Hint:

Web Site:
Username:
Email Used:
Password(s):
Notes/Security Question/Hint:

Web Site:
Username:
Email Used:
Password(s):

Notes/Security Question/Hint:

Web Site:
Username:
Email Used:
Password(s):

Notes/Security Question/Hint:

Web Site:
Username:
Email Used:
Password(s):

Notes/Security Question/Hint:

Web Site:
Username:
Email Used:
Password(s):

Notes/Security Question/Hint:

Web Site:
Username:
Email Used:
Password(s):

Notes/Security Question/Hint:

Web Site:
Username:
Email Used:
Password(s):

Notes/Security Question/Hint:

Web Site:
Username:
Email Used:
Password(s):
Notes/Security Question/Hint:

Web Site:
Username:
Email Used:
Password(s):
Notes/Security Question/Hint:

Web Site:
Username:
Email Used:
Password(s):
Notes/Security Question/Hint:

Web Site:
Username:
Email Used:
Password(s):
Notes/Security Question/Hint:

Web Site:
Username:
Email Used:
Password(s):
Notes/Security Question/Hint:

Web Site:
Username:
Email Used:
Password(s):
Notes/Security Question/Hint:

Web Site:
Username:
Email Used:
Password(s):
Notes/Security Question/Hint:

Web Site:
Username:
Email Used:
Password(s):
Notes/Security Question/Hint:

Web Site:
Username:
Email Used:
Password(s):
Notes/Security Question/Hint:

<table>
<tr><td>Web Site:</td></tr>
<tr><td>Username:</td></tr>
<tr><td>Email Used:</td></tr>
<tr><td>Password(s):</td></tr>
<tr><td></td></tr>
<tr><td></td></tr>
<tr><td>Notes/Security Question/Hint:</td></tr>
<tr><td></td></tr>
<tr><td></td></tr>
<tr><td></td></tr>
</table>

<table>
<tr><td>Web Site:</td></tr>
<tr><td>Username:</td></tr>
<tr><td>Email Used:</td></tr>
<tr><td>Password(s):</td></tr>
<tr><td></td></tr>
<tr><td></td></tr>
<tr><td>Notes/Security Question/Hint:</td></tr>
<tr><td></td></tr>
<tr><td></td></tr>
<tr><td></td></tr>
</table>

<table>
<tr><td>Web Site:</td></tr>
<tr><td>Username:</td></tr>
<tr><td>Email Used:</td></tr>
<tr><td>Password(s):</td></tr>
<tr><td></td></tr>
<tr><td></td></tr>
<tr><td>Notes/Security Question/Hint:</td></tr>
<tr><td></td></tr>
<tr><td></td></tr>
<tr><td></td></tr>
</table>

Web Site:
Username:
Email Used:
Password(s):
Notes/Security Question/Hint:

Web Site:
Username:
Email Used:
Password(s):
Notes/Security Question/Hint:

Web Site:
Username:
Email Used:
Password(s):
Notes/Security Question/Hint:

Web Site:
Username:
Email Used:
Password(s):
Notes/Security Question/Hint:

Web Site:
Username:
Email Used:
Password(s):
Notes/Security Question/Hint:

Web Site:
Username:
Email Used:
Password(s):
Notes/Security Question/Hint:

Web Site:
Username:
Email Used:
Password(s):
Notes/Security Question/Hint:

Web Site:
Username:
Email Used:
Password(s):
Notes/Security Question/Hint:

Web Site:
Username:
Email Used:
Password(s):
Notes/Security Question/Hint:

Web Site:
Username:
Email Used:
Password(s):

Notes/Security Question/Hint:

Web Site:
Username:
Email Used:
Password(s):

Notes/Security Question/Hint:

Web Site:
Username:
Email Used:
Password(s):

Notes/Security Question/Hint:

Web Site:

Username:

Email Used:

Password(s):

Notes/Security Question/Hint:

Web Site:

Username:

Email Used:

Password(s):

Notes/Security Question/Hint:

Web Site:

Username:

Email Used:

Password(s):

Notes/Security Question/Hint:

Web Site:
Username:
Email Used:
Password(s):

Notes/Security Question/Hint:

Web Site:
Username:
Email Used:
Password(s):

Notes/Security Question/Hint:

Web Site:
Username:
Email Used:
Password(s):

Notes/Security Question/Hint:

| Web Site: |
| Username: |
| Email Used: |
| Password(s): |

| Notes/Security Question/Hint: |

| Web Site: |
| Username: |
| Email Used: |
| Password(s): |

| Notes/Security Question/Hint: |

| Web Site: |
| Username: |
| Email Used: |
| Password(s): |

| Notes/Security Question/Hint: |

Web Site:
Username:
Email Used:
Password(s):
Notes/Security Question/Hint:

Web Site:
Username:
Email Used:
Password(s):
Notes/Security Question/Hint:

Web Site:
Username:
Email Used:
Password(s):
Notes/Security Question/Hint:

Web Site:
Username:
Email Used:
Password(s):
Notes/Security Question/Hint:

Web Site:
Username:
Email Used:
Password(s):
Notes/Security Question/Hint:

Web Site:
Username:
Email Used:
Password(s):
Notes/Security Question/Hint:

A

Web Site:
Username:
Email Used:
Password(s):

Notes/Security Question/Hint:

Web Site:
Username:
Email Used:
Password(s):

Notes/Security Question/Hint:

Web Site:
Username:
Email Used:
Password(s):

Notes/Security Question/Hint:

Web Site:
Username:
Email Used:
Password(s):
Notes/Security Question/Hint:

Web Site:
Username:
Email Used:
Password(s):
Notes/Security Question/Hint:

Web Site:
Username:
Email Used:
Password(s):
Notes/Security Question/Hint:

Web Site:
Username:
Email Used:
Password(s):
Notes/Security Question/Hint:

Web Site:
Username:
Email Used:
Password(s):
Notes/Security Question/Hint:

Web Site:
Username:
Email Used:
Password(s):
Notes/Security Question/Hint:

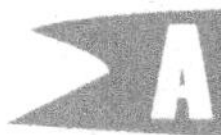

Web Site:
Username:
Email Used:
Password(s):
Notes/Security Question/Hint:

Web Site:
Username:
Email Used:
Password(s):
Notes/Security Question/Hint:

Web Site:
Username:
Email Used:
Password(s):
Notes/Security Question/Hint:

<table>
<tr><td>Web Site:</td></tr>
<tr><td>Username:</td></tr>
<tr><td>Email Used:</td></tr>
<tr><td>Password(s):</td></tr>
<tr><td></td></tr>
<tr><td></td></tr>
<tr><td>Notes/Security Question/Hint:</td></tr>
<tr><td></td></tr>
<tr><td></td></tr>
<tr><td></td></tr>
</table>

<table>
<tr><td>Web Site:</td></tr>
<tr><td>Username:</td></tr>
<tr><td>Email Used:</td></tr>
<tr><td>Password(s):</td></tr>
<tr><td></td></tr>
<tr><td></td></tr>
<tr><td>Notes/Security Question/Hint:</td></tr>
<tr><td></td></tr>
<tr><td></td></tr>
<tr><td></td></tr>
</table>

<table>
<tr><td>Web Site:</td></tr>
<tr><td>Username:</td></tr>
<tr><td>Email Used:</td></tr>
<tr><td>Password(s):</td></tr>
<tr><td></td></tr>
<tr><td></td></tr>
<tr><td>Notes/Security Question/Hint:</td></tr>
<tr><td></td></tr>
<tr><td></td></tr>
<tr><td></td></tr>
</table>

Web Site:
Username:
Email Used:
Password(s):

Notes/Security Question/Hint:

Web Site:
Username:
Email Used:
Password(s):

Notes/Security Question/Hint:

Web Site:
Username:
Email Used:
Password(s):

Notes/Security Question/Hint:

Web Site:
Username:
Email Used:
Password(s):
Notes/Security Question/Hint:

Web Site:
Username:
Email Used:
Password(s):
Notes/Security Question/Hint:

Web Site:
Username:
Email Used:
Password(s):
Notes/Security Question/Hint:

Web Site:

Username:

Email Used:

Password(s):

Notes/Security Question/Hint:

Web Site:

Username:

Email Used:

Password(s):

Notes/Security Question/Hint:

Web Site:

Username:

Email Used:

Password(s):

Notes/Security Question/Hint:

Web Site:
Username:
Email Used:
Password(s):
Notes/Security Question/Hint:

Web Site:
Username:
Email Used:
Password(s):
Notes/Security Question/Hint:

Web Site:
Username:
Email Used:
Password(s):
Notes/Security Question/Hint:

Web Site:
Username:
Email Used:
Password(s):
Notes/Security Question/Hint:

Web Site:
Username:
Email Used:
Password(s):
Notes/Security Question/Hint:

Web Site:
Username:
Email Used:
Password(s):
Notes/Security Question/Hint:

Web Site:
Username:
Email Used:
Password(s):

Notes/Security Question/Hint:

Web Site:
Username:
Email Used:
Password(s):

Notes/Security Question/Hint:

Web Site:
Username:
Email Used:
Password(s):

Notes/Security Question/Hint:

Web Site:

Username:

Email Used:

Password(s):

Notes/Security Question/Hint:

Web Site:

Username:

Email Used:

Password(s):

Notes/Security Question/Hint:

Web Site:

Username:

Email Used:

Password(s):

Notes/Security Question/Hint:

Web Site:

Username:

Email Used:

Password(s):

Notes/Security Question/Hint:

Web Site:

Username:

Email Used:

Password(s):

Notes/Security Question/Hint:

Web Site:

Username:

Email Used:

Password(s):

Notes/Security Question/Hint:

Web Site:
Username:
Email Used:
Password(s):
Notes/Security Question/Hint:

Web Site:
Username:
Email Used:
Password(s):
Notes/Security Question/Hint:

Web Site:
Username:
Email Used:
Password(s):
Notes/Security Question/Hint:

Web Site:
Username:
Email Used:
Password(s):
Notes/Security Question/Hint:

Web Site:
Username:
Email Used:
Password(s):
Notes/Security Question/Hint:

Web Site:
Username:
Email Used:
Password(s):
Notes/Security Question/Hint:

Web Site:
Username:
Email Used:
Password(s):
Notes/Security Question/Hint:

Web Site:
Username:
Email Used:
Password(s):
Notes/Security Question/Hint:

Web Site:
Username:
Email Used:
Password(s):
Notes/Security Question/Hint:

Web Site:
Username:
Email Used:
Password(s):
Notes/Security Question/Hint:

Web Site:
Username:
Email Used:
Password(s):
Notes/Security Question/Hint:

Web Site:
Username:
Email Used:
Password(s):
Notes/Security Question/Hint:

Web Site:
Username:
Email Used:
Password(s):
Notes/Security Question/Hint:

Web Site:
Username:
Email Used:
Password(s):
Notes/Security Question/Hint:

Web Site:
Username:
Email Used:
Password(s):
Notes/Security Question/Hint:

Web Site:
Username:
Email Used:
Password(s):
Notes/Security Question/Hint:

Web Site:
Username:
Email Used:
Password(s):
Notes/Security Question/Hint:

Web Site:
Username:
Email Used:
Password(s):
Notes/Security Question/Hint:

Web Site:
Username:
Email Used:
Password(s):
Notes/Security Question/Hint:

Web Site:
Username:
Email Used:
Password(s):
Notes/Security Question/Hint:

Web Site:
Username:
Email Used:
Password(s):
Notes/Security Question/Hint:

Web Site:
Username:
Email Used:
Password(s):
Notes/Security Question/Hint:

Web Site:
Username:
Email Used:
Password(s):
Notes/Security Question/Hint:

Web Site:
Username:
Email Used:
Password(s):
Notes/Security Question/Hint:

Web Site:
Username:
Email Used:
Password(s):
Notes/Security Question/Hint:

Web Site:
Username:
Email Used:
Password(s):
Notes/Security Question/Hint:

Web Site:
Username:
Email Used:
Password(s):
Notes/Security Question/Hint:

Web Site:
Username:
Email Used:
Password(s):
Notes/Security Question/Hint:

Web Site:
Username:
Email Used:
Password(s):
Notes/Security Question/Hint:

Web Site:
Username:
Email Used:
Password(s):
Notes/Security Question/Hint:

Web Site:
Username:
Email Used:
Password(s):
Notes/Security Question/Hint:

Web Site:
Username:
Email Used:
Password(s):
Notes/Security Question/Hint:

Web Site:
Username:
Email Used:
Password(s):
Notes/Security Question/Hint:

Web Site:
Username:
Email Used:
Password(s):

Notes/Security Question/Hint:

Web Site:
Username:
Email Used:
Password(s):

Notes/Security Question/Hint:

Web Site:
Username:
Email Used:
Password(s):

Notes/Security Question/Hint:

Web Site:
Username:
Email Used:
Password(s):
Notes/Security Question/Hint:

Web Site:
Username:
Email Used:
Password(s):
Notes/Security Question/Hint:

Web Site:
Username:
Email Used:
Password(s):
Notes/Security Question/Hint:

Web Site:

Username:

Email Used:

Password(s):

Notes/Security Question/Hint:

Web Site:

Username:

Email Used:

Password(s):

Notes/Security Question/Hint:

Web Site:

Username:

Email Used:

Password(s):

Notes/Security Question/Hint:

Web Site:
Username:
Email Used:
Password(s):
Notes/Security Question/Hint:

Web Site:
Username:
Email Used:
Password(s):
Notes/Security Question/Hint:

Web Site:
Username:
Email Used:
Password(s):
Notes/Security Question/Hint:

Web Site:
Username:
Email Used:
Password(s):
Notes/Security Question/Hint:

Web Site:
Username:
Email Used:
Password(s):
Notes/Security Question/Hint:

Web Site:
Username:
Email Used:
Password(s):
Notes/Security Question/Hint:

Web Site:
Username:
Email Used:
Password(s):
Notes/Security Question/Hint:

Web Site:
Username:
Email Used:
Password(s):
Notes/Security Question/Hint:

Web Site:
Username:
Email Used:
Password(s):
Notes/Security Question/Hint:

Web Site:
Username:
Email Used:
Password(s):
Notes/Security Question/Hint:

Web Site:
Username:
Email Used:
Password(s):
Notes/Security Question/Hint:

Web Site:
Username:
Email Used:
Password(s):
Notes/Security Question/Hint:

Web Site:
Username:
Email Used:
Password(s):
Notes/Security Question/Hint:

Web Site:
Username:
Email Used:
Password(s):
Notes/Security Question/Hint:

Web Site:
Username:
Email Used:
Password(s):
Notes/Security Question/Hint:

NOTE:

NOTE:

NOTE:

NOTE:

NOTE:

NOTE:

NOTE:

Made in the USA
Monee, IL
07 July 2026

56552669R00066